SIMPLE
HAWAIIAN
COOKERY

COMPILED BY EDNA BEILENSON

AND WITH DECORATIONS

BY RUTH MCCREA

Peter Pauper Press

MOUNT VERNON · NEW YORK

To the Reader

You are welcome to the Islands
Where the pace is calm and slow,
Where they dance the hula hula
And the balmy breezes blow.

We know you'll like the flavor
Of the dishes cooked with soy;
But you've got to be a native
To appreciate the *poi!*

We hope you'll have a luau
When next you entertain;
Make believe you're in Hawaii
With the palms and sugar cane!

So quickly turn the pages —
The recipes are great;
And we'll gaily sing the praises
Of our lovely Fiftieth State!

THE EDITOR

The Hawaiian Luau

For a Hawaiian Luau party, decorate with fish-net, fruits and flowers, and have the women guests wear muu-muus or grass skirts. The feast may be served on a mat on the floor, Hawaiian-style, outdoors on a picnic table, or indoors on a dining table. Hurricane lamps or candles will lend to the romantic atmosphere. Table decorations may be of sea-shells and bamboo. Play Hawaiian background music to set the mood.

Embrace each guest upon arrival, and place a lei gently around his neck. You may make the leis of artificial flowers (crepe-paper or tissue paper, or pastel facial tissue) or you may use real flowers. String flowers alternately with short sections of drinking straws to make a forty-inch necklace, using your imagination and good taste for color combinations and harmony.

Bank your Punch Bowl with flowers, and make a fruit punch to which you can add good Rum, if desired. Give the toast in Hawaiian! "Lea Lea Kakou" means "To Happiness!"

Start your party deliciously with a good seafood dip with crackers, or chilled shrimp served with a tangy cocktail sauce. End it with a Hula Sweet — pineapple chunks sprinkled with brown sugar, dotted with butter and broiled lightly. Pineapple may be wrapped in a hula skirt (aluminum foil, cut into fringes) if desired.

Make your Luau as simple or as elaborate as you wish. Remember, although the Luau in Hawaii has a religious significance, we use the name to mean "A Hawaiian Party."

Luau Menu

HAWAIIAN FRUIT PUNCH

ASSORTED RUMAKI

CREAM OF CRAB SOUP

CHINESE CHICKEN OR DUCK

ORIENTAL PEAS   SWEET POTATOES

WAIKIKI COCOANUT PIE

TEA OR COFFEE

Hawaiian Fruit Punch

1 cup canned tropical-fruit punch
2¼ cups unsweetened pineapple juice
2½ cups orange juice
½ cup lemon juice
Confectioners' sugar
1 tablespoon mint, finely chopped

In 2-quart pitcher, combine punch and juices. If desired, add confectioners' sugar to taste.

To serve: Add fresh mint, and pour over cracked ice in tall glasses. Serves 8.

Assorted Rumaki

18 slices bacon
6 chicken livers
12 water chestnuts
12 bite-size bits of fresh pineapple

Preheat the oven to 375°. Slice the bacon and chicken livers in half. Wrap ½ bacon slice around each chicken liver half and around each water chestnut and each piece of pineapple.

Arrange the rumaki on a rack in a pan and bake until the bacon is crisp, about 20 minutes. Drain on absorbent toweling and serve immediately. Serves 12.

Cream of Crab Soup

2 tablespoons butter
1 tablespoon flour
2 quarts milk
2 cups crabmeat, tinned or fresh
½ medium onion, grated
2 tablespoons parsley, chopped
2 tablespoons celery, chopped
Salt and pepper
1 cup whipping cream

Melt butter in top of double boiler. Add flour and blend. Add milk gradually, and onion, parsley and celery. Season to taste. Cook slowly until the soup thickens a little. Add crabmeat and cook a few minutes more. Serve with whipped cream.

Chinese Chicken or Duck

1 large chicken or duck
1 can pineapple
1 can mushrooms
½ cup soy
1 finger fresh ginger
2 or 3 cloves garlic

Cut chicken or duck into pieces for serving and marinate in soy, crushed garlic and chopped ginger for several hours. Fry in olive or peanut oil. Put in casserole and

add pineapple juice, mushrooms and strained soy.

Cook until tender. Fry pineapple slices in butter and serve with the chicken or duck.

Oriental Peas

1 (10 oz.) package frozen peas
½ cup water chestnuts, sliced
Salt and pepper
Butter

Place peas and water chestnuts on a square of aluminum foil. Season with salt and pepper and top with several pats of butter. Wrap securely in foil and bake at 350°, 1 hour, or grill 30 to 60 minutes, turning occasionally.

Hawaiian Sweet Potato

4 cups sweet potatoes, cooked
1 (9 oz.) can crushed pineapple,
   undrained
6 tablespoons melted butter
¾ teaspoon salt
Dash pepper
½ cup dry bread crumbs
2 tablespoons brown sugar
Dash cloves

Preheat oven to 375°. In medium bowl, mash potatoes; stir in pineapple, 2 tablespoons butter, salt, pepper. Turn into 1-quart ungreased casserole.

Combine the remaining butter with bread crumbs, brown sugar, and cloves. Sprinkle over potato mixture; bake 30 minutes. Makes 6 servings.

Waikiki Cocoanut Cream Pie

¾ cup sugar
4 tablespoons cornstarch
⅛ teaspoon salt
2½ cups milk
4 egg yolks
1 teaspoon vanilla (scant)
¾ cup whipping cream
1 cup grated cocoanut
Baked pie shell

Combine sugar, cornstarch, and salt. Scald milk and add dry ingredients slowly, stirring until a smooth mixture is obtained. Cook over hot water, stirring frequently. Cool mixture and gradually stir in yolk. Cook over hot water until custard thickens. Cool, add vanilla, and pour into a baked pie shell. Whip cream and spread over the custard. Sprinkle with grated cocoanut. Serves 6 to 8.

The First Course

Banana-and-Bacon Bits

4 bananas
¼ cup soy sauce
1 tablespoon honey
10 slices bacon, cut in half

Peel bananas; then cut into 1-inch chunks. Combine soy sauce and honey in a shallow baking dish; marinate banana chunks at least 30 minutes. Then wrap each undrained chunk with half a bacon slice; fasten with wooden pick. Brush with soy-sauce mixture remaining in baking dish; arrange on rack in shallow, open pan.

Broil about 4 inches from heat 7 to 8 minutes, or until bacon is crisp. Makes 20 hors d'oeuvres.

12

Spinach Soup with Pork

2 pounds spinach
1 clove garlic
7 cups boiling water
1 tablespoon salad oil
1/2 cup lean pork, sliced
2 1/4 teaspoons salt
1 tablespoon soy

Remove tough stems from spinach and wash leaves thoroughly. Add the soy and 1/4 teaspoon salt to the pork. Heat the oil, add the mashed garlic and pork, and fry for 3 minutes.

Remove garlic. Add the boiling water, 2 teaspoons salt, and simmer for 10 minutes. Add the spinach and simmer for 5 minutes. Serve hot. 8 servings.

Bird's Nest Chicken Soup

3 ounces bird's nest
3 egg whites
1/2 teaspoon boiled ham, chopped
3 cups chicken stock
1 teaspoon gourmet powder
1/2 teaspoon salt
3 teaspoons cornstarch

Soak bird's nest in water, 1 hour, then boil 1 hour in enough water to cover.

Wash in cold water and drain. Heat chicken stock, add bird's nest, salt and gourmet powder. Bring to a boil. Add beaten egg whites, stir constantly. Slowly add cornstarch which has been made into a paste. Stir well and cook 2 minutes. Pour in a bowl and sprinkle ham on top.

Celery Cabbage and Shrimp Soup

1 medium head celery cabbage
6 water chestnuts
1 cup canned shrimp
1 teaspoon salad oil
6 cups boiling water
1 teaspoon salt
4 scallions, chopped fine

Cut cabbage crosswise into 1-inch strips. Wash, peel and cut water chestnuts crosswise into 1/4-inch slices. Drain shrimp, saving liquid. Heat the oil until very hot, add shrimp, and fry for 2 to 3 minutes. Add the shrimp liquid, water chestnuts, 6 cups water, and salt.

Bring to boiling point and simmer for 1/2 hour. Add cabbage and boil for 15 minutes until cabbage is just tender. Add scallions and serve hot. Serves 8.

Cheese Soup

1 quart milk
2 tablespoons butter
2 tablespoons flour
1 cup soft cheese, grated
Salt and paprika
Dash Tabasco
1 tablespoon parsley, finely chopped

Heat milk in double boiler. Blend flour and butter and mix until smooth with some of the warm milk. Return to double boiler and cook for 5 minutes. Add cheese and stir until melted. Beat until smooth.

Season with salt, paprika and Tabasco. Sprinkle with a little parsley on top of each serving.

Bamboo-Shoot Soup

4 thin slices boiled ham
1½ (13¾ oz.) cans chicken broth
½ (5 oz.) can bamboo shoots,
   sliced, drained
½ (10 oz.) package frozen peas
¼ teaspoon salt

About 20 minutes before serving, cut ham into ½-inch lengthwise strips. Then combine all the ingredients in a saucepan and simmer, uncovered, 15 minutes. Serves 4.

Red Bean Soup, Hawaiian

2 cups red beans
1 small onion, sliced
1 clove garlic, cut fine
1 large potato
1 tablespoon shortening
Salt and pepper
Paprika and cayenne
1 can tomato sauce
2 quarts water
2 tablespoons lemon juice
1 small cabbage
½ cup macaroni

Cook beans in plenty of water until done. Add onion, garlic, diced potatoes, salt, pepper, shortening and cook 15 minutes. Add tomato sauce and cook 5 minutes more. Add the water and lemon juice. Mix and boil until vegetables are well done. Add cabbage and macaroni and cook 15 minutes more.

Scallion Soup

1 tablespoon sesame seeds
1 pound short ribs, cut in 1-inch pieces
¼ cup soy sauce
¾ teaspoon salt
3 cups 1-inch pieces of scallions
Black pepper

Heat sesame seeds in small skillet until golden. Wipe short ribs with a damp cloth. Put them in large saucepan with 6 cups water, soy sauce, salt, and sesame seeds; simmer, covered, 1½ hours.

Remove short ribs from soup. Cut bone and fat from meat; discard. Skim excess fat from surface of soup. Return meat to soup. Add scallions, including tops; cook, covered, 10 minutes. Before serving, sprinkle with pepper. Makes enough for 4 to 6 servings.

Egg-Flower Soup

½ cup water chestnuts
1 quart chicken broth
2 eggs
Pepper, salt

Pour half a cupful of finely chopped water chestnuts into a quart of boiling chicken broth and cook for about 5 minutes. Beat the 2 eggs and pour into chicken broth, stirring slowly until small flowers are formed. Add pepper and salt to taste. Serves 4.

Poultry Roasts and Trimmings

Mandarin Chicken

½ cup barbecue sauce
½ cup orange juice
¼ cup brown sugar, packed
2 tablespoons oil
2 tablespoons flour
¼ teaspoon salt
4 cups cooked chicken, cut-up
1 (13½ oz.) can pineapple chunks, drained
½ cup water chestnuts, sliced
1 teaspoon candied ginger, chopped
Cooked rice
Macadamia nuts or almonds

Combine barbecue sauce, orange juice, brown sugar, oil, flour and salt; mix well. Cook, stirring, until mixture comes to a boil and thickens slightly. Add chicken, pineapple, water chestnuts and ginger; cover and simmer 10 minutes. Serve over rice and sprinkle with nuts. Serves 8.

Chinese Chicken

3 broilers (2 lbs. each), split lengthwise
  in half
Salad oil
1½ tablespoons cornstarch
1½ tablespoons cold water
¾ cup sugar
¾ cup soy sauce
⅜ cup vinegar
2 cloves garlic, minced
½ teaspoon monosodium glutamate
½ teaspoon ginger, ground
¼ teaspoon pepper, cracked
6 pineapple rings

Coat chicken with salad oil. Broil skin side up, 5 inches from heat, about 20 minutes. Combine cornstarch and water; add sugar, soy sauce, vinegar, garlic, and seasonings; cook, stirring constantly until sauce thickens. Place chicken halves skin side up in shallow baking pan; pour the sauce over.

Bake uncovered in 350° oven about 1 hour, basting with the sauce several times.

About 20 minutes before serving, place a pineapple ring beneath each chicken wing; baste thoroughly, so that chicken remains juicy. Serves 6.

Chicken in Pineapple Shells

2 pineapples
2 tablespoons salad oil
1 cup onion, minced
2 cloves garlic, minced
4 cups seasoned cooked white rice
Salt
½ cup bottled barbecue sauce
Breast from 2 chickens, boned, skinned
4 teaspoons honey
4 teaspoons sesame seeds

On day before, cut pineapples in half lengthwise. Discard hard core; remove meat; refrigerate pineapple shells and meat. Sauté onion and garlic in oil until golden; add rice and ¾ teaspoon salt, then toss. Refrigerate.

About 1 hour and 15 minutes before serving, start heating oven to 350°. Fill pineapple halves with rice mixture; spoon barbecue sauce over each. Cut each breast of chicken in half lengthwise. Set a half breast on each pineapple half; sprinkle each with ¼ teaspoon salt; place in roasting pan; add ½ inch water.

Bake pineapple 45 minutes; then spread with honey and sprinkle with sesame seeds; bake 15 minutes. Serves 4.

Chicken Amandine

1 chicken, cut up for frying
1 egg, slightly beaten
1 cup fine crumbs
1 teaspoon salt
¼ teaspoon thyme
¼ teaspoon marjoram
¼ teaspoon paprika
Fat for frying
1 cup pineapple juice
2 tablespoons lemon juice
1 tablespoon cornstarch
¼ teaspoon curry powder
1 tablespoon sugar
Almonds, sliced

Dip chicken pieces in egg, then roll in crumbs mixed with salt, thyme, marjoram and paprika. Fry in ¼ inch hot fat in a skillet until brown. Drain fat from pan. Combine juices, cornstarch, curry powder and sugar. Pour over chicken. Cover.

Cook slowly 20 to 30 minutes, or until tender. Arrange pieces on a hot platter. Pour sauce over chicken and sprinkle with almonds. Serves 4-5.

Instead of almonds, Macadamia nuts may be used for a real Hawaiian flavor. Chop Macadamia nuts coarsely.

Curried Chicken

½ large fowl
2 large green peppers
1 large onion
5 teaspoons curry powder
1 clove garlic, crushed
1 teaspoon salt
½ teaspoon sugar
1 teaspoon rice wine
5 cups water

Chop green peppers and onion very fine. Crush garlic. Clean and cut chicken into small pieces; fry in a hot, greased skillet with curry 3 minutes. Add peppers, onion, garlic, salt, sugar, wine and water. Cover and bring to a boil, then turn flame low and allow to simmer 45 minutes.

Chicken Luau

1 fowl (4-5 lbs.)
Salt
Butter
2 cups milk
2 cups fresh cocoanut, grated
Flour
3 pounds spinach, cooked

Cut fowl as for stewing. Cook until tender. Season with salt and butter. Mix the milk and cocoanut and boil in a double boiler. Strain.

Make a gravy with the cocoanut milk, slightly thickening with flour. Pour over fowl. Serve with spinach. Serves 6.

Chicken Oahu

1 broiler (2½-3 lbs.)
¼ cup flour
½ teaspoon salt
¼ cup butter
1 No. 2 can (2½ cups) pineapple chunks
2 tablespoons brown sugar
1 teaspoon ginger
¼ teaspoon salt
1 eight oz. can (1 cup) seasoned tomato
  sauce
¾ cup chicken broth

Combine ¼ cup flour and ½ teaspoon salt; dredge chicken in mixture. Brown slowly in butter. Drain pineapple, reserving ½ cup syrup. Mix pineapple, reserved syrup, sugar, ginger, and salt; add to chicken. Stir in tomato sauce and broth.

Simmer covered 20 minutes. Uncover; cook 25 minutes. Salt to taste. Serve with rice. Serves 4.

Chicken Hawaiian

(Simplified)

1 large green pepper, cut in strips
1 to 2 cloves garlic, minced
2 tablespoons salad oil
2 cans cream of chicken soup
1 (13 oz.) can pineapple tidbits with juice
2 cups cooked chicken, cubed
2 tablespoons soy sauce
3 cups cooked rice
1/4 cup toasted almonds, slivered

In saucepan, cook green pepper with garlic in oil until tender. Blend in soup and pineapple juice; add chicken, pineapple tidbits, and soy sauce. Heat, stirring now and then. Serve over rice. Top with almonds. 6 servings.

Chinese Squabs

8 ten-ounce squabs
1 cup soy
3 tablespoons ginger root, finely chopped
3 teaspoons sugar
3 teaspoons Gin
3/4 cup water

Clean squabs but do not cut them up. Combine all the other ingredients in a large kettle, heat them to the boiling point, add the squabs, cover the kettle, and simmer 30 minutes until the squabs are tender. Turn squabs several times while cooking. Serve hot. Serves 8.

Shrimp Baked in Cocoanut

1½ pounds raw shrimp
2 teaspoons salt
¾ cup light cream
1 (3½ oz.) can flaked cocoanut

On the day before, remove shells but not tails from shrimp; then devein them. Sprinkle with salt, then refrigerate. Pour cream over cocoanut; refrigerate.

About 45 minutes before serving start heating oven to 350°. Arrange shrimp in 13 x 9 x 2-inch baking dish; sprinkle moist cocoanut, lifted from cream, on top; pour on cream. Bake 40 minutes. Serves 8.

Shrimp Kabobs

Cooked shrimp
Stuffed olives
Pineapple chunks
Barbecue sauce

Arrange shrimp, olives and pineapple on skewers. Grill or broil, brushing with barbecue sauce and turning often.

Baked Shrimp Hawaiian

3 pounds deveined shrimp, uncooked
Dash cayenne
2 tablespoons prepared mustard
1 teaspoon brown sugar
1 tablespoon steak sauce
1/2 cup melted butter
3 drops liquid hot-pepper seasoning
1 teaspoon salt
1/2 cup fresh bread crumbs, buttered

Preheat oven to 375°. In boiling water to cover, simmer shrimp, with cayenne, 5 minutes. Drain, and dice. Arrange in baking dish. Combine mustard, brown sugar, steak sauce, butter, hot-pepper seasoning, and salt. Spread over shrimp; sprinkle with buttered bread crumbs. Bake 15 to 20 minutes, or until crumbs are golden. Serves 6.

South Seas Shrimp Salad

2 bunches scallions
1 1/2 pounds fresh spinach
2 (4 1/2-oz. size) cans cooked shrimp, drained
1/4 cup soy sauce
1/4 cup salad oil
Dash pepper

Trim green tops from scallions; chop tops fine. Wash spinach, and shred; put in salad bowl. On top of greens, pile chopped onion tops, then shrimp. Arrange onions spoke fashion around salad.

In a jar with tight-fitting lid, shake soy sauce, salad oil, and pepper to combine thoroughly; use as dressing for salad. Makes 6 to 8 servings.

Hauoli Fish Barbecue

2 cups soft bread crumbs
2 cups drained cucumber, chopped
2 eggs, beaten
½ cup onion, chopped
¼ cup melted margarine
Salt and pepper
1 trout or whitefish (4-6 lbs.),
   cleaned and boned
Bottled barbecue sauce
Canned pineapple slices
Ripe olives

Combine bread crumbs, cucumber, eggs, onion, margarine and seasonings; mix well. Stuff the fish; skewer it together.

Place stuffed fish on aluminum foil and brush generously with barbecue sauce. Wrap securely in foil and grill 1 hour or bake at 350°, 2 hours. Garnish with pineapple slices and olives. 8-10 servings.

Fried Rice with Lobster

1 egg
1 small lobster
2 cups cooked rice
1 teaspoon soy sauce
½ teaspoon gourmet powder
1 teaspoon canned French
  mushrooms, diced
1 peeled water chestnut, diced
1 teaspoon canned bamboo shoots,
  diced
Dash pepper

Boil lobster 10 minutes. Remove meat
and dice. Cook the same way as "Fried
Rice." (See page 50). When putting rice
in skillet, add lobster, mushrooms, water
chestnut and bamboo shoots.

Fried Rice with Shrimp

1 egg
2 cups cooked rice
½ cup shrimp, cooked
1 teaspoon soy sauce
½ teaspoon gourmet powder
Dash pepper

Boil fresh shrimp about 5 minutes and
remove shells. Cut shrimp in half, remove the veins, then dice. Cook the same
way as "Fried Rice." (See page 50).

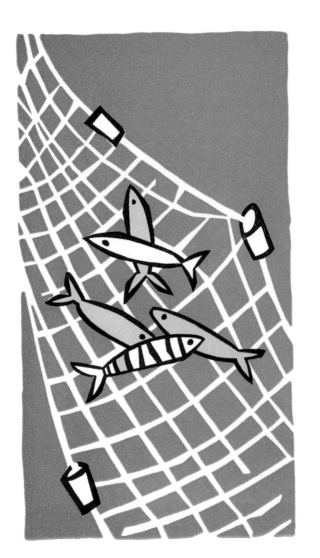

Luau Lobster

4 lobster tails, cooked
1 (1 lb. 4½ oz.) can pineapple tidbits
  drained
1 cup barbecue sauce
1 cup celery, sliced
Parmesan cheese, shredded

Remove meat from lobster tails, leaving shell intact, and cut into bite-sized pieces. Combine lobster, pineapple, barbecue sauce and celery; fill shells and sprinkle with cheese. Wrap each securely in aluminum foil and grill 20 minutes.

Polynesian Bundle-Bake

3 cups hot cooked rice
¼ cup margarine
1 cup cooked ham, cubed
1 cup pineapple chunks
1 cup green pepper, thinly sliced
½ cup barbecue sauce

Combine rice and margarine; toss lightly. Add ham, pineapple, green pepper and barbecue sauce; mix well. Place individual servings of the rice mixture on squares of aluminum foil, bring corners together and twist. Grill or bake at 350°, 20 minutes. 6 servings.

Oriental Pork

1 tablespoon shortening
1 pound lean pork, loin or shoulder
1 teaspoon salt
2 teaspoons Worcestershire sauce
2 teaspoons lemon juice
1 tablespoon brown sugar
2 medium onions, sliced
1 (13½ oz.) can pineapple tidbits
1 green pepper, cut into strips
1 envelope curry sauce mix
½ cup cold water

Heat shortening in skillet. Cut pork into ½-inch slices; cut slices into 2-inch strips. Brown lightly in hot shortening, about 5 minutes. Sprinkle with salt. Add Worcestershire sauce, lemon juice, sugar and onion slices. Drain liquid from pineapple into a measuring cup. Add water to make 1¾ cups. Pour over pork and stir, bringing to a boil.

Cover; reduce heat; cook gently 20 minutes. Add green pepper. Continue to cook 2 or 3 minutes. Meanwhile combine envelope of curry sauce mix with cold water. Push meat to one side of pan, add curry mixture, stirring constantly. Mix all together. Bring to boiling point. Serve hot over rice. Serves 4.

LAMB

Pork Chops, South Seas

4 loin pork chops
Salt and pepper
Flour
4 slices canned pineapple
4 pitted prunes
4 carrots
1/3 cup water

NO FAT ADDED

NASZPIKOWAĆ
CZOSNKIEM

Wipe chops and season with salt and pepper. Dust with flour, and place in pan. Upon each chop place a ring of pineapple with a pitted prune in the center. Between chops, place whole carrots, and add water.

Cover. Cook slowly for 1½ hours. Remove to hot platter. Make a gravy from mixture in pan. Pour over chops. Garnish with parsley. Serves 4.

Hawaiian Ham Kabobs

Cooked ham, cut into cubes
Pineapple chunks
Green pepper, cut into squares
Barbecue sauce

Arrange ham, pineapple and green pepper on skewers. Grill or broil slowly, brushing generously with barbecue sauce and turning frequently.

Pork with Watercress

1½ pounds loin pork chops
2 tablespoons salad oil
1 onion, sliced
2 cloves garlic, finely chopped
¼ teaspoon ginger, ground
2 bunches watercress, stems removed
1 teaspoon cornstarch
2 teaspoons soy sauce

Remove bone from pork chops and pound meat to ½-inch thickness. Cut flattened pork into inch-wide strips; then cut each strip into 1½-inch pieces. Heat oil in large skillet. Add onion, garlic, and ginger; sauté, covered but stirring occasionally, about 5 minutes. Add pork; cook, stirring 15 minutes, or until well done. Add watercress; cook, covered and over low heat, 10 minutes.

Meanwhile, combine cornstarch and 1 tablespoon water; mix until smooth. Stir cornstarch mixture and soy sauce into pork and watercress; bring to a boil; then cook, stirring, 1 minute, or until thickened. Serve hot over fluffy white rice. Serves 4.

Rib pork chops may be used instead of the loin chops, but they are less meaty.

Oriental Pork and Beans

2 (1 lb.) cans pork and beans,
   with tomato sauce
1 (12 oz.) can luncheon meat
4 to 6 pineapple slices
2 tablespoons brown sugar
1 teaspoon prepared mustard
1 teaspoon Worcestershire sauce

Put beans in shallow 12 x 8 x 2-inch baking dish. Slice meat into 6 or 8 pieces; place in center of beans in overlapping slices. Cut pineapple slices in half; arrange around meat in scallops.

Make a paste of remaining ingredients; spread over meat and pineapple. Bake in a moderate 375° oven about 20 minutes or until beans are bubbling. Makes 4 to 6 servings.

Baked Spare-Ribs

Lean spare-ribs
Dry mustard
Cloves
Salt and pepper
Brown sugar
1 clove garlic
Butter

Rub spare-ribs on both sides with garlic.

Dot widely with cloves. Sprinkle with salt and pepper. Then rub on mustard; spread thickly with brown sugar. Dot with butter and put in medium oven to bake. Turn and baste until done.

Roast Loin of Pork

3½-pound loin of pork
2 tablespoons crystallized ginger,
  finely chopped
¼ cup soy sauce
Watercress

Preheat oven to 325°. Make several small slits at intervals in pork. Insert in slits 1 tablespoon chopped ginger. Combine rest of ginger and soy sauce. In shallow roasting pan, arrange pork loin, fat side up. Brush pork with part of soy-sauce mixture.

For well-done roast, cook pork about 1 hour and 45 minutes, brushing with soy-sauce mixture several times during roasting. Remove from oven; wait 20 minutes; then carve.

To serve: Put pork loin on wooden board or serving platter; garnish with watercress. Makes 6 to 8 servings.

Tropical Ham

1 canned ham (11-12 lbs.)
Whole cloves
1 pound brown sugar
2 cups Burgundy
1 cup canned pineapple juice
Thin orange slices
Thin lime slices
Prepared mustard

About 3 hours before serving, stand ham upright, on its broad end in a large roasting rack. Remove all gelatin from ham. Then, with a sharp knife, make diagonal cuts, 1/8 inch deep and about 1 inch apart, across all but back and bottom surface of ham. Repeat these cuts, at an angle, to make a series of diamonds. Then, on front side of ham, place a whole clove in the center of each diamond.

Heat oven to 350°. In large shallow roasting pan, on a rack, place ham, back side down. Pat all surfaces with brown sugar.

In large bowl, combine 1 cup brown sugar, Burgundy, pineapple juice; set aside 1 cup of this sauce. Now bake ham 2 hours, basting ham occasionally with some of remaining sauce. Then remove ham from oven and increase oven heat to 450°.

Stand ham on its bottom surface in the pan, brush top and sides with rest of remaining wine sauce; pat with brown sugar. Return to oven for 5 minutes, until brown sugar is melted and ham glazed.

Remove from oven. Garnish with orange and lime slices, secured with toothpicks, then set on large wooden cutting board or platter. Serves 12 generously.

Celery Cabbage and Pork

1 medium head celery cabbage
6 water chestnuts
4 scallions
¾ cup pork, ground
1 egg yolk
¾ teaspoon salt
6 cups boiling water

Cut cabbage crosswise into 1½-inch strips. Wash, peel, and cut water chestnuts in cross sections ¼-inch thick. Chop scallions very fine and mix with the pork, then add egg. Combine salt, boiling water, and water chestnuts; cook for 15 minutes.

Add cabbage and cook until nearly tender. Drop the pork a teaspoonful at a time, into the soup. Boil for 5 minutes and serve hot. Serves 8.

Glazed Pork Chops

6 thick loin pork chops
2 cups brown sugar
½ cup unsweetened pineapple juice
½ cup honey
2 teaspoons dry mustard
6 whole cloves
12 whole coriander seeds, crushed
Orange, lemon, and lime, sliced

Brown chops in pan; season with salt and pepper, then place in shallow baking dish. Combine remaining ingredients and spoon about 3 tablespoons over each chop. Bake uncovered in 350° oven, 1¼ hours, basting now and then with rest of sauce.

With toothpick, peg a slice each of orange, lemon, and lime on every chop, top with Maraschino cherry; baste fruit with sauce and bake 10 minutes longer. Arrange on leaf-lined platter. Makes 6 servings.

Curry Aloha

1 cocoanut, grated
4 cups milk
1 tablespoon onion, chopped
2 tablespoons butter
1 tablespoon curry powder (scant)
1 teaspoon ginger, ground
Fish, chicken or lamb

Grate cocoanut and soak in milk for 1 hour. Fry onion in butter until brown, then add to the onion the curry and the ginger. Strain off the milk from the cocoanut, and pour it over the mixture in the frying pan. Put in the raw chicken, fish, or meat and cook slowly until done.

Serve with salted peanuts, grated cocoanut, chutney, preserves or finely chopped bacon, fried crisp.

Island Burgers

Ground beef
Barbecue sauce
Syrup from pineapple
Round buns, split and toasted
Pineapple slices
Tomato wedges
Stuffed olives

Shape beef into patties and marinate in equal parts of barbecue sauce and pineapple syrup; drain. Brush generously with sauce and grill or broil with pineapple slices.

For each serving, place a hamburger on the bottom half of a bun and top with a pineapple slice. Garnish with tomato wedge and olive.

Sweet Potatoes Oahu

Cooked sweet potatoes, sliced
Bananas, cut diagonally into 1-inch pieces
Pineapple tidbits
Margarine
Brown sugar
Miniature marshmallows
Macadamia nuts or almonds

For each serving, place potatoes, bananas and pineapple on a square of aluminum foil. Dot with margarine and sprinkle with sugar. Wrap securely in foil. Grill 15 to 20 minutes. Top with marshmallows and nuts.

Fried Broccoli

3 cups cooked broccoli, chopped
4 teaspoons olive oil
$\frac{2}{3}$ teaspoon garlic, finely chopped
$\frac{1}{3}$ teaspoon salt
Dash pepper

Parboil broccoli in 2 cups water to which $\frac{1}{2}$ teaspoon salt has been added. Cut broccoli in pieces $\frac{1}{2}$-inch long. Heat olive oil and fry the garlic until it begins to brown. Add the broccoli and fry until it is thoroughly heated. Stir mixture frequently, season, and serve immediately. Serves 6.

Skillet Beans

8 slices bacon
5 slices pineapple
2 (1 lb.) cans pork and beans
2 tablespoons brown sugar

Cook bacon in skillet until crisp; drain on paper towel; crumble coarsely. Pour off all but 2 tablespoons drippings; sauté pineapple until lightly browned; remove. Combine beans, brown sugar, and crumbled bacon in skillet; heat through. Top with pineapple slices; heat until bubbly. Makes 5 servings.

Island Fruit Salad

1 cup crushed pineapple
1/2 cup golden seedless raisins
2 cups pineapple chunks, well drained
2 cups celery, diced
1 cup mayonnaise

Drain crushed pineapple well, reserving syrup. Add raisins to syrup and heat just to boiling; remove from heat and let stand 10 minutes to plump raisins; drain. Mix pineapple chunks, celery, and drained raisins. Combine crushed pineapple and mayonnaise; add to salad and toss lightly. Chill. Arrange on lettuce. Serves 6.

47

Boiled Rice

1 cup rice
1½ cups water

Wash rice thoroughly in several changes of water, until the water comes clear. Put rice in pot, add the 1½ cups water and boil 5 minutes with lid off; turn the flame lower and let the water boil off. Turn flame to lowest point, put on lid and heat 20 minutes. A crust should form at the bottom, but it should not burn.

Outrigger Rice

½ cup onion, chopped
¼ cup margarine
4 cups cooked rice
1 (13½ oz.) can pineapple tidbits,
  drained
½ cup seedless raisins
1 teaspoon salt
1 teaspoon curry powder
1 teaspoon oregano

Sauté onion in margarine. Stir in remaining ingredients. Form square of aluminum foil into boat shape and fill with rice mixture. Grill or bake at 350°, 20 minutes. 6-8 servings.

Fried Rice

1 egg
2 cups cooked rice
½ cup roast pork, diced
1 teaspoon soy sauce
½ teaspoon gourmet powder
1 scallion, chopped
Dash pepper

Scramble egg in a hot, greased skillet until slightly brown. Add scallion, roast pork and rice. Sauté 2 minutes, add soy sauce, gourmet powder and pepper. Cook another 2 minutes.

Orange Rice

(Simplified)

3 tablespoons butter
1 cup celery with leaves, diced
2 tablespoons onion, chopped
2 tablespoons orange rind, slivered
2 cups orange juice
2 cups pre-cooked rice
¾ teaspoon salt
⅛ teaspoon thyme

Melt butter in deep saucepan. Add celery and onion; cook until onion is tender, but not brown. Stir in orange rind and juice;

bring to a boil. Add cooked rice, salt and thyme; mix just enough to moisten all the rice.

Remove from heat; cover and let stand 5 minutes. Fluff with fork before spooning into center of crown roast of pork, or serve with baked ham or Hawaiian-style chicken.

Macaroni Sai Men

1 package macaroni
1 bunch scallions
1 large can mushrooms
5 slices bacon
1 tin tuna
Soy to taste

Cook macaroni. Cut scallions into 1/2-inch pieces. Fry chopped bacon and white part of scallions. Add mushrooms and 1/4 cup soy and 1/4 cup juice from mushrooms. Cover and steam for 5 minutes.

Add green tops of scallions, tuna, macaroni, and more soy and mushroom juice if needed. Steam, covered, over low heat for 20 minutes. Serve in bowls with a crisp green salad.

This makes an interesting luncheon dish, or one-course dinner.

Desserts and Pastries

Baked Bananas in Sherry Sauce

6 bananas
Lemon juice sauce
2 eggs
4 tablespoons sugar
4 tablespoons Sherry
2 egg whites
1 cup whipped cream
Rind of 2 lemons, grated

Peel ripe bananas and cut in half lengthwise. Arrange in buttered casserole and squeeze lemon juice over them. Let stand for ½ hour. Cover with sauce and bake in 350° oven for 25 minutes, and serve piping hot.

Sauce: Beat egg yolks, add sugar, and beat again. Add Sherry, 2 egg whites which have been well-beaten, whipped cream and grated lemon rind.

Bananas Baked in Orange Juice

6-8 medium bananas
1 medium orange, peeled and cut
  in chunks
2 tablespoons orange juice
2 tablespoons lemon juice, fresh,
  frozen, or canned
1/3 cup sugar
Dash cinnamon
Dash nutmeg

Preheat oven to 325°. Peel bananas and arrange in shallow baking dish. Add remaining ingredients. Bake 25 to 30 minutes, or until bananas are golden and tender. Serve hot or cold.

Bananas Baked in Wine

5 bananas
1/2 cup brown sugar
3/4 teaspoon cinnamon
1/2 cup white wine

Preheat oven to 350°. Peel and slice bananas lengthwise in half. Arrange halves in a greased shallow baking dish. Sprinkle with a mixture of brown sugar and cinnamon. Pour wine over fruit and bake for 15 to 20 minutes or until golden brown.

Royal Cocoanut Cream Pie

1 cup milk
1 1/3 cups sugar
Pinch of salt
2 egg yolks, beaten
2 tablespoons cornstarch
1 tablespoon milk
2 1/2 teaspoons gelatin, dissolved in
    1 tablespoon milk
1/2 cup cocoanut
1 cup cream, whipped
1 teaspoon vanilla
2 egg whites, beaten
1 baked 10-inch pastry shell

Combine milk, sugar, and salt in saucepan and bring to a boil. Blend cornstarch and the milk and mix with yolks of eggs. Add to hot milk above and cook slightly.

Dissolve gelatin in 1 tablespoon milk and pour hot mixture over it. Let set until firm. Put in electric beater and beat well.

Add cocoanut, whipped cream, and vanilla to above mixture and put in refrigerator for 10 minutes. Fold in stiffly beaten egg whites; pour in baked pastry shell; cover with whipped cream and sprinkle with cocoanut.

Tropical Cheese Tarts

Pastry
4 eggs
½ cup sugar
⅛ teaspoon salt
1 cup milk
1 teaspoon vanilla
1 cup fine cottage cheese
1 cup flaked cocoanut

Line 3-inch tart pans with pastry. Beat eggs in top of double boiler. Add sugar, salt, milk. Place over boiling water, and cook, until thickened, stirring constantly.

Remove from heat, and add vanilla. Fold in cheese and cocoanut; pour into prepared pans. Bake in hot oven, at 425°, for 15 to 18 minutes, or until done. Makes 12 tarts.

Pineapple Mousse

1 (20 oz.) can crushed pineapple
1½ pints heavy cream, whipped
1 teaspoon lemon juice

Drain the crushed pineapple and fold carefully into whipped cream. Add lemon juice, cover and freeze in refrigerator overnight. Do not stir. Serves 10.

Papaya Freeze

1 cup sugar
1/2 tablespoon lemon juice
1 1/2 cups orange juice
1 cup papaya pulp
2 cups rich milk

Mix sugar, fruit juices and papaya pulp and chill thoroughly; gradually stir into milk and freeze in an ice cream freezer. If papaya is out of season, use 1 cup papaya marmalade and omit sugar. Serves 8.

Prune Pie

1 1/2 cups pineapple juice
1 pound dried prunes
1 tablespoon melted butter
1 teaspoon cinnamon
1/2 cup brown sugar, firmly packed
1/2 teaspoon nutmeg
1/4 teaspoon salt
1 teaspoon orange rind, grated
1 unbaked pastry shell

Add pineapple juice to prunes; let stand overnight. Simmer until prunes are tender; remove prune pits. Add butter, sugar, cinnamon, nutmeg, salt and orange rind.

Set in pastry shell and bake in 425° oven 35-40 minutes.

Tropical Gingerbread

1 cup shortening
½ cup sugar
2 eggs, unbeaten
½ cup molasses
1⅓ cups flour
½ cup cold water

1 cup grated cocoanut
1 teaspoon soda
1 teaspoon ginger
1 teaspoon cinnamon
¼ teaspoon salt

Cream shortening and sugar, add eggs. Beat together. Dissolve soda in molasses and add to first mixture. Mix and sift dry ingredients and add to the molasses and egg mixture alternately with cold water.

Stir in the cocoanut. Pour into a well-greased pan and bake in a moderate oven for 35 minutes. Sprinkle with powdered sugar and cocoanut.

Pineapple Ambrosia

2 large pineapples
1 package frozen mixed fruits, thawed
3 bananas
½ cup light Rum
¼ cup flaked cocoanut

Day before, halve each pineapple down center lengthwise. Scoop out meat, then cut up the meat. Refrigerate both shells and meat.

At serving time, toss pineapple meat with mixed fruits and bananas, sliced thin; spoon into pineapple shells, which have been arranged on a platter; spoon Rum over fruit mixture. Garnish top with flaked cocoanut.

Hawaiian Cookies

1/2 cup butter
1 (3 oz.) package cream cheese
1 teaspoon vanilla
1 cup sugar
2 eggs
2 1/4 cups flour
2 teaspoons baking powder
1 teaspoon soda
1/2 teaspoon salt
1 (8 1/2 oz.) can crushed pineapple,
   well drained
1/2 cup chopped Maraschino cherries,
   well drained
1/2 cup nuts, chopped

Blend together butter, cream cheese and vanilla; add sugar and mix well. Add eggs, one at a time, beating well after each addition. Gradually add sifted dry ingredients; mix thoroughly. Stir in pineapple, cherries and nuts. Drop by rounded teaspoonfuls onto greased cookie pans. Bake at 350°, 15 minutes. 4 dozen cookies.

Hot Cocoanut Soufflé

⅓ cup quick-cooking tapioca
⅓ cup granulated sugar
2 cups milk
3 eggs, separated
2 tablespoons butter
1 (3½ oz.) can flaked cocoanut
¾ teaspoon lemon extract
¼ teaspoon salt
3 tablespoons flaked cocoanut
Whipped cream, flavored with
  Sherry or Rum

In double boiler combine tapioca and sugar; add milk, then cook over boiling water about 10 minutes, stirring occasionally until thickened. Meanwhile, beat egg yolks until thick and light in color. Remove tapioca mixture from heat. Stir in 2 tablespoons butter, can of cocoanut and extract.

Beat egg whites until foamy. Add salt and beat until stiff but not dry. Into cocoanut mixture lightly fold yolks until blended; turn into large bowl. Fold in whites. Turn into prepared casserole. Sprinkle with 3 tablespoons flaked cocoanut.

Bake 45 minutes. Serve immediately with whipped cream flavored with Sherry or Rum. Makes 6 servings.

Ap. 57